WHAT IS THE STRUCTURE OF A PLANT?

LOUISE SPILSBURY

Britannica
Educational Publishing

IN ASSOCIATION WITH

ROSEN
EDUCATIONAL SERVICES

Published in 2014 by Britannica Educational Publishing (a trademark of Encyclopædia Britannica, Inc.) in association with The Rosen Publishing Group, Inc.
29 East 21st Street, New York, NY 10010

Distributed exclusively by Rosen Publishing.
To see additional Britannica Educational Publishing titles, go to rosenpublishing.com.

First Edition

Britannica Educational Publishing
J.E. Luebering: Director, Core Reference Group
Anthony L. Green: Editor, Compton's by Britannica
Mary Rose McCudden: Editor, Britannica Student Encyclopedia

Rosen Publishing
Hope Lourie Killcoyne: Executive Editor
Nelson Sá: Art Director

Library of Congress Cataloging-in-Publication Data

Spilsbury, Louise
 What is the structure of a plant? / Louise Spilsbury. — First edition.
     pages cm. — (Let's find out! Life science)
Audience: Grades 3 to 6.
Includes bibliographical references and index.
ISBN 978-1-62275-251-5 (library binding) — ISBN 978-1-62275-254-6 (pbk.) — ISBN 978-1-62275-255-3 (6-pack)
1. Plant anatomy — Juvenile literature. 2. Plants — Juvenile literature. I. Title.
QK49.S7165 2014
571.3'2 — dc23
                                    2013026806

Manufactured in the United States of America.

Photo credits
Cover: Istockphoto: Borchee fg, HuePhotography bg. Inside: Dreamstime: Bogdanwanko 23, Evan66 28, Maksudkr 7, Marilyna 26–27, Mikeexpert 6–7, Rtimages 27, Sangiorzboy 25, Sippakorn 24, Tanchic 22, Toliknik 21; Istockphoto: Borchee fg, HuePhotography bg; Shuttterstock: 19, 20, BlueRingMedia 16, Joy Brown 9, Lucian Coman 29, Feoktistoff 4, FocalPoint 12, Yuriy Kulik 5, Lzf 14, Mycola 15, Kotenko Oleksandr 13, Leena Robinson 17, Roundstripe 11, Anna Subbotina 8, Jiri Vaclavek 18–19, Andre Viegas 10.

CONTENTS

About Plants

The grass we run on, the trees that tower above our heads, and the colorful flowers that brighten our yards look very different, but they are all plants. There are plants all over the world. They live in hot, warm, and cold places. Plants grow in dirt, in water, and even on other plants! Plants are living things, just like us. They grow, feed, and reproduce.

Plants range in size from big trees to tiny mosses that live on tree trunks.

A water lily is a type of plant that lives in water.

THINK ABOUT IT

As you read this book, try to find the patterns plant parts follow. For example, what do all roots, stems, and flowers have in common?

Plants come in different sizes, shapes, and colors, but most types are made up of the same basic parts. Most plants have roots, stems, leaves, flowers, and fruit. Each part of a plant must do a certain job to help the plant survive and grow new plants.

Roots

We cannot usually see roots because they grow under the ground. Roots hold plants in the ground. They help stop plants from being blown down by the wind.

Roots are covered in tiny hairs. Water and nutrients from the soil soak into the root hairs and travel up the roots to the rest of the plant. Plants need water and nutrients to live and grow.

▶▶ **Roots suck up rainwater that washes into the soil.**

Different plants have different types of roots. Some plants have many small roots that grow in different directions. Other plants have one big root called a taproot that is firm and tough. The taproot grows straight down into the soil.

COMPARE AND CONTRAST

Plants make their own food, and some plants store this food in their roots. Radishes and carrots are roots that store food. Why do you think we eat these roots and not others?

STEMS

Stems are plant parts that usually grow above the ground. A stem is the stalk from which buds, shoots, and leaves grow. Stems have hollow tubes inside them. These work like drinking straws. They carry water and nutrients up from the roots to the other parts of the plant.

THINK ABOUT IT

The water that travels up the tubes inside a stem helps the stem to stand up. How do you think a stem would be affected if a plant did not get enough water?

>> Some bamboo stems can grow up to 1 foot (0.3 m) every day!

There are all sorts of different stems. Plants can have one stem or many. Some plants' stems have thorns. Many stems are straight and firm. Others are thin, floppy, and not strong enough to stand up by themselves.

Thin, floppy clematis stems cling to objects, such as fences, for support.

TRUNKS

Tree stems are very thick, tall, and strong. They are called tree trunks. Trees have strong stems so they can hold up heavy branches that grow leaves and flowers. Tree trunks are covered in a tough outer layer called bark. Bark is like a suit of armor that protects the tree trunk inside.

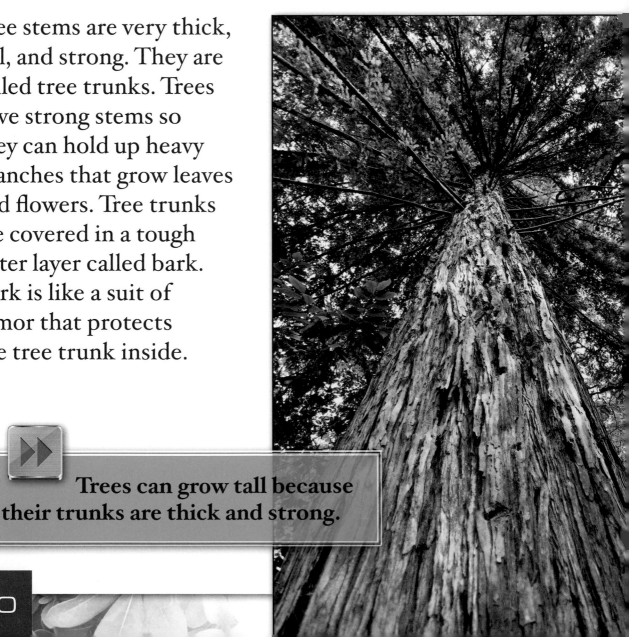

>> Trees can grow tall because their trunks are thick and strong.

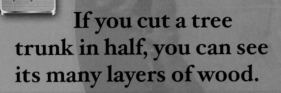

If you cut a tree trunk in half, you can see its many layers of wood.

THINK ABOUT IT

Trees usually grow one layer of new wood each year. When a tree is cut down, you can see the layers as circles. These are called tree rings. How could you use tree rings to figure out the age of a tree?

Tree trunks are made of a sturdy plant material called wood. A tree grows by producing new layers of wood around the trunk, just under the bark. Over time, the wood in the middle of the tree dies and becomes hard. This makes the trunk strong.

LEAVES

Leaves come in many different sizes, shapes, and colors, but they all have an important job to do. Leaves make food for plants by a process called photosynthesis. They use energy from sunlight to turn water and air into food. Water travels from the roots of a plant to its leaves. Air moves into leaves through little holes in the bottom of the leaves.

Energy is the power that can make things work, move, live, and grow.

▶▶ The lines on this leaf are veins that carry water and nutrients through the leaf.

Stems hold up leaves. They also spread out leaves so they can get as much light as possible. Plants use the food made in leaves to grow and to make other plant parts.

Some trees drop their leaves in fall. Their leaves stop making food and then fall to the ground. The trees rest in winter and store energy to grow new leaves in spring.

▶▶ Leaves change color when they stop making food.

SPECIAL LEAVES

Most plants have wide, flat leaves to catch more sunlight. Some plants have special leaves that are long and thin. These leaves are called needles or spines.

The spines on cactus plants are a type of leaf. Cactus plants make food in their green stems, not their leaves. Cactus plants use their sharp leaves to stop animals from eating their stems.

Cactus spines are an unusual type of leaf.

Trees such as pines and firs have needle leaves. These needles can make food. They are a special shape to help them survive the cold. Needles are not damaged by snow and ice. They stay on the tree through the winter.

COMPARE AND CONTRAST
How are the long, thin spines of cactus plants and the needles of fir trees the same? How are they different?

Needle leaves can stay on a tree all year round.

FLOWERS

Most, but not all, plants grow flowers. Like leaves, flowers come in many sizes, shapes, and colors. Flowers grow the seeds that many plants use to reproduce. Most flowers have petals. Inside the petals are male parts called stamens, a female part called a pistil, or both. Stamens hold a powder called pollen. When pollen is moved from a stamen to a pistil, that flower can start to grow seeds.

Stamen

Petal

Pistil

Bees help some flowers transfer their pollen.

Some flowers make a sugary drink called nectar. They often have colorful petals that attract insects or small birds. When these animals visit flowers to drink nectar, pollen rubs onto their bodies. When the animals visit a new flower, the pollen rubs onto its pistil. This is called pollination. Once a flower has been pollinated, it can begin to grow seeds.

FRUITS

When a flower has been pollinated, its seeds begin to grow. Fruits grow around the seeds to protect them. Some fruits, such as oranges, are soft, juicy, and sweet. Other fruits, such as nuts, are hard and dry. Some fruits contain one seed, while others have many seeds.

THINK ABOUT IT

What do all fruits have in common? Why do you think they help to move seeds away from the parent plant?

The fruit of the poppy plant is hard and dry and has many seeds inside.

Fruits help to move seeds. After an animal eats fruit, the seeds come out in its droppings. Squirrels and chipmunks gather nuts and bury them to eat later. Some of these nuts are forgotten, and when their hard fruit cases rot away, the seeds grow.

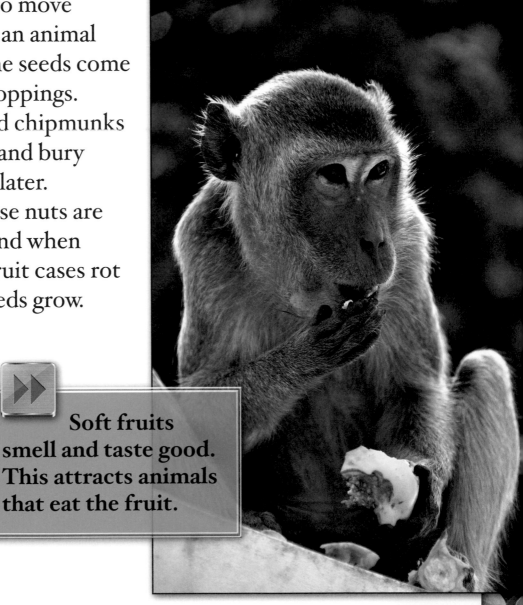

Soft fruits smell and taste good. This attracts animals that eat the fruit.

CONES

Some trees and shrubs, called conifers, grow cones instead of flowers and fruit. Cones are made up of overlapping scales. Seeds grow between the scales. The scales of the cone get thicker, darker, and harder as the seeds under them grow bigger.

▶▶ Pine cones change from small and green to big and brown as their seeds grow bigger.

A **conifer** is a plant that grows cones. Most conifers have leaves shaped like needles.

Cones release seeds onto the ground to grow new conifers.

Like fruits, cones help seeds move away from the parent plant. When conifer seeds are fully grown, the cone releases them. Some cones open their scales in dry weather and the seeds fall out. Other cones have scales that fall off, taking their seeds with them. Once the seeds are on the ground, they start to grow into new conifers.

SEEDS

Seeds are structures that can grow into new plants when they leave the parent plant. Seeds come in all sorts of shapes and sizes. Some flowers make thousands of seeds so tiny you can hardly see them. A seed from a coconut tree is huge and can weigh around 4.5 pounds (2 kg). Every seed contains the parts it needs to grow into a new plant.

We eat some seeds. Peas are seeds that grow inside a fruit called a pod.

Around a seed is a hard layer called the seed coat. This layer protects the seed until it is ready to grow. Inside the seed are an **embryo** and food. This food keeps the embryo alive until the seed is ready to grow.

First, roots and stems grow from a seed. Then, the plant grows leaves, too.

An **embryo** is a partly developed plant inside a seed. An embryo grows into a plant.

SPORES

Some plants, like ferns and mosses, make spores instead of seeds. Ferns and mosses release their spores, which then grow into new plants just like the parent plants.

Fern spores are very tiny. They are contained in packets on the underside of fern leaves. When the spores are ready to grow, they fall from the plant. Spores grow in damp places. They cannot grow easily if it is dry and hot.

Packets of spores can be seen on the bottom of a fern leaf.

Spores

Spores

Moss plants release spores from packets at the top of their stalks.

THINK ABOUT IT
Ferns and mosses produce millions of spores. Why do you think they do this? How might this help their chances of growing new plants?

Mosses are soft, small plants that grow on damp rocks, tree trunks, and forest floors. Mosses grow stalks with packets of spores at the top. In dry weather, when the spores are ready to grow, the packets open and the spores blow away.

Bulbs

Some plants make parts called bulbs. Bulbs can grow into new plants. They grow underground. Bulbs are made up of layers of thick, overlapping leaves that grow around a bud. The bud contains the tiny parts needed to grow a new plant.

A **bud** is a small swelling on a plant that contains the shoot, leaf, or flower of a new plant.

Bulbs that we can eat include onions and shallots.

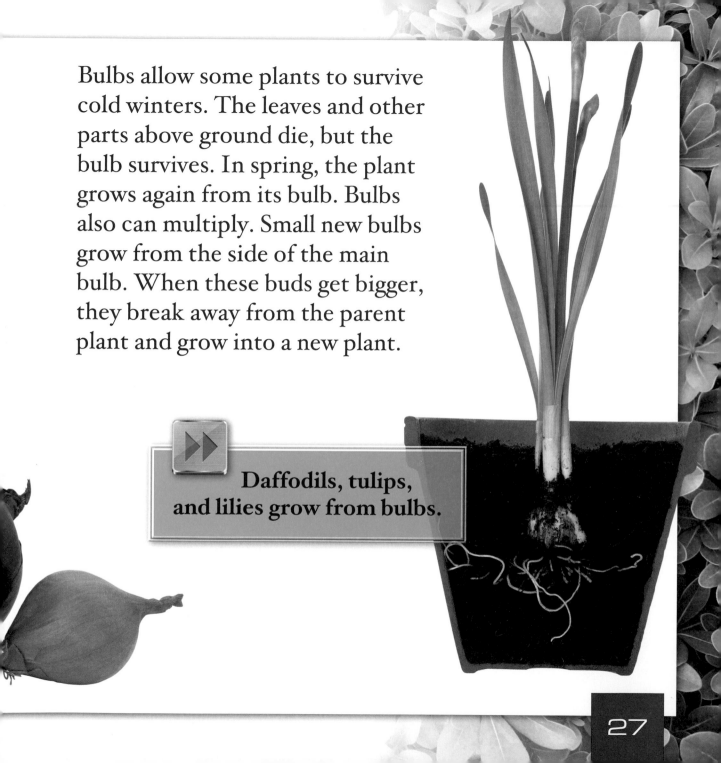

Bulbs allow some plants to survive cold winters. The leaves and other parts above ground die, but the bulb survives. In spring, the plant grows again from its bulb. Bulbs also can multiply. Small new bulbs grow from the side of the main bulb. When these buds get bigger, they break away from the parent plant and grow into a new plant.

Daffodils, tulips, and lilies grow from bulbs.

GROWING WELL

Plants grow well only in the right conditions. When there is too little water, a plant wilts or droops, and may die. When leaves do not get enough light, they cannot make food, so the plant cannot grow properly. Some plants need shade and die if planted in areas that get a lot of sunshine.

THINK ABOUT IT
What do all plant structures have in common? What pattern have you noticed they follow?

Plants wilt if they do not get enough water.

Each part of a plant has an important job to do. Roots provide plants with water and hold them in the ground. Leaves make food for the plant. Flowers, fruits, and cones make seeds to grow new plants. With enough water, nutrients, and light, the different parts of a plant work together to form a healthy plant.

Glossary

bark The tough outer layer of a tree trunk.

bulbs Buds surrounded by thick overlapping leaves that can be planted.

conditions The environment surrounding something.

hollow Having an empty space inside.

nectar A sugary juice found inside the middle of a flower.

nutrients The food that plants and animals need to grow and keep healthy.

parent plant The plant from which the seed of a new plant comes.

pistil The female part of a flower.

pollen A powder that is found inside a flower that causes plants to grow seeds.

pollination The act of moving pollen from a stamen to a pistil.

roots The parts of a plant that grow into the soil.

seed coat The hard layer around a seed.

spores The reproductive parts of some plants, such as ferns and mosses.

stamens The male parts of a flower that contain pollen.

stem The central part of a plant.

taproot A large main root that grows straight down.

tree rings The layers of wood that grow on a tree's trunk each year.

FOR MORE INFORMATION

Books

Burnie, David. *Eyewitness Plant* (DK Eyewitness Books). New York, NY: DK Publishing, 2011.

Kalman, Bobbie. *Plants Are Living Things* (Introducing Living Things). New York, NY: Crabtree Publishing Company, 2007.

Lynette, Rachel. *Plants* (Raintree Perspectives: The Science Behind). North Mankato, MN: Raintree, 2013.

Stewart, Melissa. *How Does a Seed Sprout?: And Other Questions About Plants* (Good Question!). New York, NY: Sterling Children's Books, 2014.

Veitch, Catherine. *Learning About Plants* (The Natural World). North Mankato, MN: Raintree, 2013.

Websites

Due to the changing nature of Internet links, Rosen Publishing has developed an online list of Websites related to the subject of this book. This site is updated regularly. Please use this link to access the list:

http://www.rosenlinks.com/lfo/plant

Index